THE ART OF RESTORATION

KAREN KILCUP

Winter Goose
PUBLISHING

Winter Goose Publishing
45 Lafayette Road #114
North Hampton, NH 03862

wintergoosepublishing.com
Contact Information: info@wintergoosepublishing.com

The Art of Restoration

Cover Picture "Nude and Rocks" by Charter Weeks

Cover Design and Formatting by Winter Goose Publishing

ISBN: 978-1-952909-26-9

Published in the United States of America

To the Skimmilk Farm writers

CONTENTS

PRIME NUMBER

Divisible only by itself
and one, sixty-seven's
a funny number.
Like the fritillaria,
checkered lily,
like the frilled white dress
whose neckline plunged, revealing
nothing at my senior prom,
like primal scream therapy,
now out of fashion.
Another funny number,
my insurance agent calls
to say I'm nearly
there, wherever there
is. Perhaps it's climbing
a mountain, a Sisyphus
with just one chance.
Or maybe it's the top
and I roll down, a cool zero
at the bottom, a snow woman
with coal eyes and parsnip nose.
I imagine gaunt men
in a windowless room
at MIT spinning billions
of calculations per second.
Sorry, I tell them,
my family's always
beat the odds,
lived past ninety.
My lover says
I'm in my prime,
juicy as a rib roast
bad for one's heart
but oh so tender.

Oh, Divine One,
let me be primordial
as a shark, primary
as a mountain goat;
let me be a milkweed pod
split in autumn air
whose silky filaments drift
past counting.

I. MOTHERS AND OTHER
STRANGERS

LIVING IN A SPLIT, 1959

Like a figure in my paint-by-numbers kit,

I'd loll on the spotless cotton couch, between
        frosting-pastel lamps seemingly squeezed
                from pastry tubes, their dusty shades

stitched with silver. They always came in pairs.
        A house away, my sitter Sheila stacked up
            45s, gushy how-I-love-you

songs, a black whirlpool. My best friend Cindy P.,
        not ashamed of being fast or smart, opened
            her mother's kitchen drawer,

withdrew a ten-inch knife, and hissed
        she wanted to slit me.

Who was home at this hour? My father still
        had hair. At night his huge hands caressed
            the upright piano's keys like a lover
                unlocking

a forbidden door. A room away, my red-lipped silent
        mother sliced steak as if her life depended
            on it. She never told me not to play

with strangers. The TV asked, *What does it mean to be*
        an American? Outside, mushrooms bloomed like
            bombs. Above the backyard grill, clouds

smeared a painter's oily sky. Flamingos were not pink.

WHAT HAPPENED IN FIFTH GRADE

In music class I realized my voice
was always flat. The nurse spelled out
what periods meant (we thought them only
dots that ended sentences)—the dormant
egg erupts then sticks in darkness
so thick you wouldn't dare close your eyes.
As if in proof, my beautiful young teacher
changed her name, got fat, then suddenly surly—
for talking too much I had to stand out
in the hollow hall
with Denny Eaton, class cut-up.
Class brownie gone bad.

One day as we giggled through
a stupid movie, our erect principal snapped on
the lights—*The President has been shot
and is dead.*

I still can see my test
with the word *concieve*
marked with a pincurl *correct.*
I can't remember if I told the truth.

SWIMMING AT THE SALT MARSH

Cousin, you always feared the water,
but I was older, though just a girl.
Even blinking made you sweat,
your face a morning pond-bottom
scarred by turtle trails.
My scarlet Keds were warm on pavement scored
by horses' hooves, as puddles shimmered
ahead, and around the corner by White's Bridge
the marsh unfurled, the river rising
to our nostrils like the gargle
my mother gave for sore throat.

Off the road, we'd sink to our ankles
in dark brown muck,
sawgrass striping our legs red.
You shuddered— *Are there bloodsuckers?*—
as the river creased and foamed.
Shells lay on edge deep beneath the surface,
but I'd plunge off the bank into
the fizz, hollering
scaredy cat before you'd drop too, suspended
until you let your breath go.

I remember Mother's tale
of jumping off the arching bridge,
remember how it ended—
a broken bottle slit her foot open.
I still see the hole, the shape
of her lipsticked mouth
when she said *no.*

REFLECTIONS

Say It With Rubies,
Flame Red, Passion Pink, Firecracker,
Moonglow Mauve, Inkberry Stain, Fire and Ice.
Seven silver cylinders, your lipsticks lured me.
I remember you leaning in—gilt-edged
silver oval carved with leaves
and flowers, it captures
your young face,
hazel eyes,
in a lake
of light.

Now I lift your mirror,
envision you combing a tide
of tangled tawny hair in which my father
surely found himself at sea. Once, ashore
in Korea, he sent me aqua watered-silk pajamas so shiny
I could see myself, or so it seemed.
Looking in your glass
I found the dragon
on my back.

ALONE IN DEEP

The fair child finds herself alone
in a supermarket aisle,
she clasps the pebbled
brightness of a lemon, it hurts

her eye, she remembers its sour
heart. Where is her mother?
The waxed floor mirrors morning,
it's a frozen lake, thin ice she'll

break through with her next step. Where is
her mother? The fair child cannot
recall her father, an absence
filled with brittle weekend smiles

and shouts. He's a blanket, a light
snapped off, an untold bedtime story.
She finds herself alone in deep
grass bordered by black woods. Inside,

she's an island silence: unseen
insects ticking, a squirrel's random
scold, his tail like Barbie's evening
boa. Trees stretch up and down like bars.

The sun's lodged in the sky like a
rock. The wind carries animal
voices her mother has told her
are hungry. Where is her mother?

SPACES

No cheerful nurse, just hard
chairs and stale book smell, as we
waited for his hunched welcome before
the examination.
Every spring she handed me over
to the hands that smacked my backside,
and the square loose face that loomed
like God's the time that water filled
my lungs and fever blistered
all my dreams.
My lovely mother—dark-haired, red-lipped,
always gleeful in her cherry
Mercury rag-top—hushed and flattened
here, like a poppy pressed between
thick handmade pages.

He'd carefully arranged the room—
acutely-angled scissors bloomed
from the lip of a stainless bowl,
the smooth white sheet that covered
the table was not disposable.
An exhibition of body parts
(were they even human?)
floated in jars around the edge.
I'd try not to look at their pinkness.

That day the dry grip raised me to my feet.
As she looked on, her face serene,
he sat down, gray wool suit awry,
his legs splayed apart at my waist.
His breath funneled from the black caves
of his nose, warmed my cheek and brow.
He unzipped my flowered pants and plunged
his thick hairy finger into places
for which I had no words,

and probed and spun until my tongue
thickened and my throat closed.

Whose heart was suspended
in that jar behind my back?
What stories did she and he exchange?

I remember that after,
she talked to him as if in prayer
to the father she always said she never had.
I can still feel his fingers press
my breasts, my mouth.
I never wanted to touch
the space he left behind.

GOING UNDER
for Stephanie

Sunny spectacled father in the photos
        he holds her bone-white face;
                her aggie eyes see everything, nothing.

At five, she thinks she's fully dressed
        with cowboy hat, bullet-studded holster,
                pearly-handled gun. When she falls

from the spotted pony he's so proud she's mastered,
        it crushes her forearm with its arched hoof.
                In a white gown under a white sheet

in a white room full of women's voices, she hears
        a white-masked man who straps her down.
                He says he doesn't mean to hurt her,

holds an ether-soaked gauze over her nose and mouth.
      She dreams she is an angel, she can fly
                away. Back home in bed she hears

someone breathing in her closet through pleated skirts.
        If she covers her head, holds her breath,
                and shuts her lids, he'll recognize

tonight she's dead. Behind her eyes her mother wears
        a ruby dress and strand of pearls.
                Sleep funnels her toward school,

the Visible Man and Visible Woman, private parts erased;
        plastic layers lift from skin
                to muscle, rainbow organs, white frame.

Surprised one morning coming from his closet,
        he meets her eye level with his drooping
                pink bone. His hands curve over

her buttocks in punishing love, forbidding gaze.
        That night she watches
             a chip of moon arc

over his heaving shoulder; it's a hook, a knife
        she can't yet reach. Her aggie eyes see nothing,
           everything.

On a hidden horizon, the sun oozes. In a bay, tight-lipped
        oysters embedded in sand cover secret grit.
           Full moon, pearl button, fastens

midnight's blue-black blouse.

GONE ROGUE

In middle school   our hygiene teacher
     Mrs. Miller warned   the girls
about rogue sperm—   they infest
          all the swimming pools
and ponds, they   inhabit the shower
     (*don't take one after your brother*),
they live on soap and   don't give up.
I felt lucky to be   an only child.

Getting birth control   in a popup clinic,
I'm in the stirrups,   and the doctor knows
   I'm nervous, so he tells me   one woman's cure
          for yeast—a yogurt douche, only
she used blueberry   instead of plain,
     and when he checked her the berries
oozed out.   For some reason
          this story does not   amuse me
     as it does the doctor and the woman
     who helps him, whom I believe
is a nurse.   But he helps me,
          and I'm glad they come
     to an unmarked house   and labor
          in someone's living room
for free.   They do not ask why
     I'm there,   or what I need.
Exceptions   were the rule.

Today the headlines track
old news—   heartbeat laws,
     reimplanting ectopic fetuses,
          consensual rape.
     Today I'm grateful
I have no daughters,   no granddaughters.
          For menopause.

FAMILY PLOT

"You have more to fear from the living than from the dead."
—traditional family saying

How fortunate these ghosts are old—
guarded by granite posts
and rusty cast-iron chains
lush with poison ivy,
the cemeteries keep all the ancestors
safely down. A stranger maintains
the Stumpfield plot, rakes leaves each fall,
but the ground edges over
the broken stones that every year
become less legible.

In the bird-filled woods we struggle
to see dementia, death from drink,
babies felled by dysentery,
memorialized by initials in tiny stones.
These losses reincarnate
in our thinning generations.
Here the stones occlude
such hard facts.

But the virtues remain.
In memory of Enoch Gove,
born Oct. 10, 1764, died Dec. 3, 1828,
aged 64 years.
In labour industrious,
in business, upright,
and a friend to the
widow and fatherless.
In society retiring,
but a patriot true
to his country.
In friendship, largely known

and deeply loved.
And in faith, he died with hope in Jesus Christ.

The only tales stones tell, they tell in soundless song—
He is gone, forever gone,
And left each dear familiar spot;
Love may invoke, with tenderest tone
His name, but he cometh not.

SUPPLY COMPANY

My mother sold plumbing and heating for a living, bolstering her home building business—odd for a woman in the fifties—so she could buy wholesale. Up front she staged aqua tubs and toilets, vanities in rainbow colors along with Johnny-rings, plungers, black-and-white boxes (like TVs those days) bearing products with names I couldn't pronounce. She did the books but loved the *merch*, though my dad sold too and costed plans for the baggy plumbers who slouched in at seven a.m. opening. One employee, an alcoholic uncle, arrived by motor scooter, sun or snow. Mother (never Mom) let him put an old clawfoot tub in the plate-glass showroom window and fill it with soil. He planted tomatoes, sweet during the winter doldrums, and a Sensitive Plant that drew kids whose parents came for repair advice and discount parts. The kids would crow when touching the plant's leaves made them slowly close. If they behaved, she might give them (or even me) a Squamscott Beverage lemon-lime soda from the warehouse cooler beside the crappy bathroom (Employees Only) with its orange-stained toilet bowl. Relishing contests, she fought IRS audits and the town fathers who demanded she take the rusting surplus tub and pink toilet seat off the street sign. She asked if there was anything on the sign they didn't have in their own homes, and won. In those days, business was good.

Then my dad got Parkinson's. And my uncle and his wife left for Florida. She sold the shop to a family hardware chain that folded when The Home Depot opened up the street, and retired to tend her blind horse and the last cats born on the family farm. She loved sleeping in but missed the talk and the *sell-sell-sell*. She'd hoot about the little boys who'd sometimes secretly pee in a display. On her last day she waved to the lone town cop as she planted mums before she went inside to make chowder, and die. When I sold the farm, the septic system failed inspection, and I had to install a new one. The night before they closed the gash in the ground, I sprinkled her ashes liberally, keeping some for another place, a later date.

FOREMOST BUILDERS

My mother's business sign for Foremost boasted "Homes designed for women by a woman." Single-story capes and ranches, three bedrooms, bath and a half, 1000 square feet, with walk-out patio and hardwood floors, aimed at postwar families like ours. She organized the plumbers, painters, electricians (and mason-carpenters like her father) who swarmed the projects. Decked out in a dress, never forgetting red lipstick, she'd supervise a crew, and when they finished one, we'd live there till they built the next. Serial movers. When I was barely old enough for school we got a special house, a modern split. My bedroom had a gable window only birds could use, and knee-wall windows that made you squat to look into the backyard. The landing held her office piled with paper, pencils, multiple staplers; she did the books there every night. Around the time we moved she got sick and disappeared, so I lived with her parents. A hysterectomy at twenty-eight. When she came home, she kept on working days and nights but cooked much more, elaborate multiple-course meals with butter, butter, butter that often made me sick. Sometimes for a break she'd serve a TV dinner—I loved peeling back the hot aluminum foil, steam swirling in my face as I exposed the prize—perfectly elliptical Salisbury steak, sunny corn, whipped potatoes, gravy. Much later, after my father died of Parkinson's, she cooked again in earnest, saying she was worth the best. She died stirring soup, her cat Grateful swirling around her feet. I struggle to remember and forget her.

FAMILY ALBUM

I struggle to remember and forget her. Although they're both long gone, something tangible remains—the album I discovered buried in the closet when I sold the farm. Were they ever young? One black-and-white snapshot shows my twenty-three-year-old mother upright in bed, her long brown braid hanging down her left shoulder. She kept the braid, getting grayer, till she died. The pillow propped behind her back almost engulfs her. In another, my father holds me in his arms; I am impossibly small, a preemie with a grapefruit face enclosed by a blanket that must be pink. His blond hair is wispy; it's before he's started shaving his head (*so much cooler in the summer*), and he grins as if he holds the Queen of New England. Other pictures show them on opposite ends of a pale sofa beside a glass-topped kidney-shaped coffee table, Pall Malls in hand. I finally find what I've been looking for, the one my mother told me about again and again. A friend has stopped to meet me, and when she sees me in the crib she gasps. *You let that cat sleep with the baby?* My mother has answers to every question. *That cat has a name: Mildred.*

DIFFERENTIALS

My father could do anything. He built a kitchen with a stack of three-hundred-year-old boards, dovetailing all the drawers. When snowstorms hit, he'd guide the old Ford tractor's blade to clear a perfect line two inches from the barn doors. He taught me calculus when I was twelve, the best differential equations. He knew at least a dozen knots, and tied the tightest manrope I ever saw. I taught him how to knit, and he made me an Icelandic sweater whose yoke had six soft greys, and a popcorn-stitch-adorned fisherman's cardigan rippling with double cables tight and precise as if he'd carved them. Driving back from playing contract bridge together, he'd remind me that in the fourth hand on the sixth round, I should have played low, not wasted my ace of hearts.

When I was twenty-five, he disowned me when he learned I might live with a Black man. Not long after, I married a civil engineer he liked and whom I later divorced for abuse. By then my dad's Parkinson's was bad and he kept falling. When he couldn't eat or walk, my mother found a bed nearby. Work made me move out of state, but I'd visit when I could. The nurses always told me how proud he was of what I'd done.

SECOND COUSIN

Priscilla lived life large and loved guests. To every knock on her unlocked door, she'd shout a welcome that belied her size. No lost dog went homeless. After visiting us one day, she went outside and found her blind and lame and deaf rescues panting after tearing down her battered Chevy van's headliner into festive ribbons. She shrugged and said, *bad dogs*, jumped in and drove away. Another time, Deacon, her fat old chocolate Lab, tackled me when I opened the fridge, and when I pushed him hard, she sighed.

An avid mariner, she'd shepherd me and my cousins into the retired wooden fishing boat she named the IXAT, telling us, *look in a mirror*. In a cloud of diesel fumes, we chugged through the throat of the Merrimack for dinner flounder and some salty air. Summers, she'd sleep onboard and come ashore to get groceries and give the dogs their legs.

She filled her ceramics shop from floor to ceiling using her own molds—stippled cantaloupe-shaped breakfast bowls with orange mouths, grooved yellow cassava melons for soup, oversize cabbage serving dishes, a long trout hollowed out for presenting fish. She sold them all to Saks and Nordstrom's before cheap copies arrived from China. She made me dozens of miniature animals, and I'd create a Noah's Ark parade across my Aunt Fan's floor. The rooster was as big as the silver horse.

Her unused parlor held three shelves of African violets, pink and white and purple, frilled and multiple, that like the horsehair-stuffed sofa belonged to her mother. The year my father kicked me out she welcomed me to her best bedroom and refused rent. A seventies woman in the fifties, she smelled of cigarettes and dog and clay, and I never saw her wear a dress. The Pall Malls and shop dust finally killed her. Although she planned a legacy, she left me nothing but herself.

GREAT AUNTS

One black-and-white snapshot shows me smiling slightly,
lolling on Fan's stone step, cowboy hat askew, uncontrolled
blond curls spilling out. The entry porch, thick with winter
coats resting for the summer, smelled faintly of manure and
hay that followed Uncle Leonard from the barn. The kitchen
linoleum cooled my bare feet. Fan showed me how to make
butter from the Jersey cow's cream, churning till yellow bits
congealed and we could squeeze them into thick rounds. Her
wooden mold impressed the top with a fat cow so pretty I
hated spreading her gold onto bread.

Fan's companion Lucy read us poetry in the family room—
Frost, Dickinson, Longfellow. A schoolteacher, she'd had an
education in the teens, when country women normally stayed
home. She claimed the *Boston Herald* every morning. The only
aunt who drove a car, she carried us all to church each week.
One foggy night when we were headed for a rummage sale,
she drove us off the road into a ditch. No one was hurt
except the car. It was our funny story and great adventure. I
remember someone saying once that Lucy wasn't really my
aunt, but I knew she was.

Aunt Sarah's ten-foot ceilings made even towering Uncle
Harry seem small. Her parlor yawned. A pink and green and
cream brocade-covered, horsehair-stuffed baroque sofa,
adorned with massive mahogany grapes and vines,
demanded perfect posture. The minister never stayed too
long. Against the opposing wall reared an upright piano no
one ever played. The tripartite bow window bore flowers—
four dense levels of African violets, purple, pink, lavender,
white, frilly blue, skewbald blue and white. The morning sun
pulled blooms above their hairy leaves.

All younger than I am now, they seemed forever old. They
wore flowery belted dresses, laced-up black oxfords, and

opaque cotton stockings, flesh-colored but fooling no one. They all loved to win and lose at bridge. Sarah, who died first, favored lavender toilet water. She was thin and crisp, like her ginger snaps that stung the tongue. Fan, the eldest, had wavy white hair like her mother and wore a floral apron every day. Lucy didn't know how to cook and moved out after Fan vanished when I was thirteen. My mother never told me where Fan went. The last time I visited, she couldn't remember my name.

GREAT UNCLE

In one rusty photo, the monumental Clydesdales flank him,
looming like benevolent sphinxes, their mild white faces
unmoving. He's still young; without his jaunty cap, one
might mistake him for a child. In another, he stands beside a
yoke of oxen, his slight figure firm beneath their magnificent
horns. A third image, now in color, shows us bundled up for
winter, sitting side by side on the red sulky behind my elderly
pinto pony Calico. I am four, but Len's not much bigger. He
leans slightly forward while I hold the reins and beam. He
seldom speaks but lets me help him gather eggs from the
muttering hens, filling my basket with warm brown ovals
speckled with dung. We drive the cows to and from the low
pasture. "Buttercup" is my favorite. One day he covers my
hand over the Jersey cow's teat so I can squeeze it hard
enough to squirt a string of milk into the galvanized pail,
making it ring. The cream that rises in the icebox bottle is
three inches deep. It makes the best butter.

He keeps cows well into his seventies, although he milks
them with a stainless-steel machine. When an arsonist burns
the old family barn flat one night, he loses all his cows, and
his greying hair, always a little awry, suddenly turns
completely white. His eyes are bluer than a winter sky, and
he still loves to laugh. He never finds a wife. Even without
the hens and ducks and sheep and horses and cows, he stays
a farmer all his life.

BERTHA THE SAINT

The state police saved her, called the SPCA about the big dog left behind when the nearby airbase closed. Just past a pup, she wandered through the busy traffic circle before they grabbed her. The rescue people called my mother because she had a farm with room to run and other animals for company. Barely ten, I named her Bertha because it seemed to say her softness. Winters were hers, rolling canine snow angels on the powdery lawn, heaving puffs above her head, reveling in the cold. Summers made her sprawl on grass. Soon after she arrived, we wondered why the horses wouldn't use their outdoor water trough, until we caught her one August morning stepping daintily over the rim and settling up to her neck. Later she'd swim in the nearby beaver pond. Every morning she trotted to the neighbor's house to socialize and sleep with the multiplying outdoor cats. The neighbor liked to say *Bertha's a good banker—she always leaves a big deposit.*

She tolerated our poodle Pierre, the only animal my born-poor mother ever bought. One day we saw him and Bertha moving slowly through the back field while he hauled a bloody carcass twice his size—a dead woodchuck she'd likely caught between its holes. She let him take the credit. He'd beg for hard-boiled eggs, but when we gave her one, she shuffled around the corner of the house and plopped the cold rubbery oval whole into the flower bed. She never wanted to offend.

She didn't drool much. She rarely let me leave her view, especially when we were young. Hours before a thunderstorm approached, she'd pant panic at my heels. She died as largely as she lived, swimming ashore.

FARM POODLE

He arrived when I was five and he was eight weeks old, a
corkscrew comic who quickly knew he was Pierre. He grew
into a subtle people manager, a gourmand commanding a
large vocabulary. *Would you like a hard-boiled egg?* Absolutely.
What about some chicken? Sure, but turkey would be even
better. *Was that you who got into the kitchen drawer?* I did, but I
took only one tiny bite of several milk chocolate bars. I'm
surprised you noticed. *How about some green peas?*
Disgusting! When he broke his hind leg and got a cast, he
asked to be carried up and down our steep stairs. One day
my mother left him up and when she came inside from
feeding horses, he met her at the door. Then realized his
blunder and scrambled back up and whimpered. A water dog
who hated being wet, he knew hours before a bath was
coming, ducked under the bed to evade my mother's grasp,
showing all his teeth and growling when she reached for him
(always a faker). After she washed and dried and primped
him, he begged to go outside and rocketed past the barn to
roll luxuriously in the manure pile (Better!). Despite his fancy
pedigree, Pierre was no show, all farm.

INHERITANCE

Almost sixty years ago she bought
the farm from the builder's last
descendant, a grizzled man living
with a grizzled friend in one room that housed
a single light bulb and a woodstove,
out back a four-hole outhouse. Selling
plumbing for over forty years,
she kept the seat propped up
in the barn's big loft
to remind her where and how she started.
She filled the farm with heat and light,
then packed the place—
doomed thoroughbreds too slow to race,
elegant and flighty and kind,
Great Danes and calico cats,
abandoned, crying, ribby.
Instead of fighting with me
or my father, she'd retreat to the barn—
The animals are always happy
to see you, they never complain,
you can tell them your troubles.
At last, stubborn and silent, she planned
to die alone, at home, and did,
much too young. Just dropped.
Seafood chowder on the stove,
her last cat circling, waiting
for the pink lobster scrap
she'd always share.

My mother left me
poor. The windows are rotting,
the boiler heaves and fails,
the barn roof leaks.
Her fields are closing
with oak and locust volunteers.

Without her to forbid it
I ride her '70 Ford tractor
that overheats and stalls
in the low corner of the back field
where springs surge
nearly year-round. How often
I have to call *the hook*.

These breathless summer days
the mower blade fells all,
small creatures rush from the rumble
grinding mouse and snake, blind shrew
flanked by fox and red-tailed hawk
in the dead elm.
The field's skeleton emerges
beneath fallen stalks—the farmer
who ditched this ground drew
lines of loam, unspeaking print
his last bequest.

Unsupervised at last,
I find myself
summoning the spotted ponies
buried here—
Bucky, Princess,
her favorite, Prince,
who mastered me
when I was small
and he was strong.
Bertha the Saint Bernard.
And still, the strong bones
of lovely horses—Topaz,
Pink Lady, Saturn Breeze, Go-Go,
Crying Moose, Vavite,
Vavite Encore.

MOVING
for my mother

The new folks want a clean start,
so I sell the battered tractor
that almost killed me after you died,
the lawnmower, an old barn scale,
two huge pulleys with woven rope
big as my wrist and long as the barn,
piles of two-hundred-year-old boards,
bins of strap hinges with curlicued tips;
inside, your yellow blockfront dressing table
with schoolgirl decoration, my grandmother's
room-size braided rug, your grandfather's veneer
secretary where he wrote you loving letters
when people still wrote letters;
paintings, tables, cracked China-trade
plates and bowls and cups and saucers,
a blue and yellow Delft charger repaired
with twenty-three lead staples
on the back, and—you loved these almost
as much as the years of drop-off
cats who curled in their rush
and splint and cushioned seats—
chairs, chairs, chairs, chairs, chairs.

The final sale's a silvery image I've kept
covered to shield it from the light—
an eighteen-inch square walnut frame
with gold-leaf inner edge encloses
a thick chenille-work picture oval—
lavish pink and red roses twined
with bright green leaves embracing
a studio portrait—perched on a chair,
his slim paws draped gracefully
on top, a white-bibbed tiger cat looks
alertly, cheerfully, to one side.

The caption reads "Our Tom."
The dealers who buy him promise
a good home.

Mr. Emerson claims that all returns—
Every sweet hath its sour;
every evil its good. But like you I know
some losses stay lost.

II.   LEAVES AND LEAVINGS

CATCH AND RELEASE

At Sunday dawn the ranger, God, sleeps in.
From the mountain's peak, a legend
points us to a power station, a brooch
with chain of silver smoke, the towns of Hadley
Northampton and Holyoke, and the river,
an iridescent scarf that curves around
the valley's neck.

A solitary boat wrinkles the water's silver skin,
and I see a fisherman plumbing
muddy currents: he starts with lines miscast,
snarled in branches of the everyday—
a child's cough, insurance bills, a surly boss—
and a week's work yields piles of curlicued
catfish, only good for bait. He throws them
back in bits and hopes they'll make a change
into something rich and strange, like trout.
He knows it's a fish-eat-fish world,
just as he's sure silver needles thread
beneath the surface, gills filter
what they need. Schools nibble weed,
and stragglers trace erratic patterns.
I want to tell him words lure like worms, we're
hooked on our own meanings, but that's not it
exactly. We catch or release
what we can, fathom
only what we must.

NAÏVE PORTRAIT, C. 1865

In the well-known museum
whose name eludes me now,
she hung, and may hang still,
in a carved and gilded rectangle,
her aquamarine silk dress edged
with billows of foamy eyelet,
hair falling like ebony water,
lips parted. To her right,
behind a transparent swag,
a tiny window cut
in half by a river punctuated
with white sails; black dots figure
people on the shores.
A giant swallow perches
on the sill, waiting
for a message.

But it's the eyes that speak
of worlds beyond her frame—
a husband often gone on business,
or pleasure; a sister given to drink;
an infant lost to typhoid,
or the flu. Or perhaps
the mind supplies
the gaps—a cursive letter
on her ivory-painted table,
a red rose trailing
from her hand,
a locket filled with a wave
of her lover's hair.

BOUNDARIES

You assume your usual chair
beneath the primitive portrait,
your gift to me. After a space
and time you've returned again.
Over supper, we chat about the news—
the latest bombings, the state of the union,
the bowl of limes that cost
so much. You study your plate;
I trace the lines of your face,
erasing the faulty
boundaries I've created.

Outside on the road, our steps
fill the hollow below.
Off the tar we leave erratic trails
of trampled grass between the brambles,
as gleaming Venus waxes in the west.
A voice breaks the stillness—
a solitary whippoorwill, steady
as a pulse. You clasp my hand—
He's calling for his mate.
You listen for an answer.
I pause. *I think he's only tired
of silence.*

While we wait, another joins, and then another,
until a chorus fills the space, then suddenly
the voices stop.
You press beside me, inhaling
deeply timothy hay and evening.
Then once again, the single bird
begins the trembling song,
insisting over and over
that spring has come
to stay.

PLUM ISLAND AT DUSK

Beaver Moon's orange cheek
leans against us,
raising tides, and water floods
the island's one-lane road.
The ranger checks us—
Do you know the rules?
You always say we do,
though we forgot them all
years ago. He waves us on.

Except for other lovers
of nature, we're alone;
waves skip and fall,
crest and slide.
I walk on wet sand,
you on dry.
We talk about the undertow—
it took three kids last June,
when you were gone.
I poke a rubble of shells,
seeking one unbroken.
The chambered house
of one, snail-like,
admits all eyes,
its hardness half-
missing.

Up ahead
a wispy woman
walks her dog—
he zigzags back
and forth from
hissing wave
to crumbling dune.

PAWTUCKAWAY, LATE

The park surrounds me with intelligence—
leaves rattling messages from northern borders,
hemlocks clipped to keep the pathway open,
silver beech trunks in martial file,
and boulders, lichen-green, sentinels
on the ridges.

A beaver lodge flanked by trees gnawed
through, pencil-pointed, white chips
like shattered teeth. In a frozen pond, ice
cracks—muffled gunshot
fired through sharpening air.

My glance snags on a blue whir; a jay's jagged
cries telegraph war. I seek and fail
to reach the lake my map has said lies deep
inside the wood's soft pocket. At home, under-
cover, I find black ice, find myself falling
down, falling through to numbness, then the peace
of stones, of water, of limbs bare in winter night.

Gulf War, January 18, 1991

BARN FIRE

The first flame rises, smoke
        unfurls. One snorts, another screams
            and staggers down, eyes shade

like clouds passing over water. Whiskers, unholy candles;
        a chestnut sheen consumed, fleshless
            body fallen.

The firemen's yellow coats congeal from the inferno—
        four of fifty-nine are saved.
            The awful incense lasts

for days. The witnesses sift the char,
        timber and bone, that fills the stone
            foundation hole.

Do horses dream? Cylinders of carrot in outstretched
        palms, alfalfa underfoot, still ponds at dawn?
            Rolling clover fields whose only sound

is birdsong, and quiet breath?

THE SKY IS JUST ABOUT TO FALL

Clean of ash for months, the fireplace's breathless mouth
         awaits a match. The storms have pivoted, south
            to north. Black birds disturbed

by shifts in light, in magnetism, whirl as one body
         in carnival arcs; landing, they clatter
            in shagbarks. In the quirk

of autumn thunderstorms, their cries merge with leaf-
         speckled wind. The cat scatters carcasses
            about the yard—rabbit's foot

amid asters, mouse hindquarters beneath rugosas'
         orange hips. The garden feeds the eyes
            alone—a single cherry tomato bush bears

green stones that never ripen. In these elongating
         months, the ones with an R, a growl, I wake
            to find you gone to dig for oysters,

as if we're going to starve. Mornings on the marsh
         teams of hunters in camouflage slog
            through fog, lugging guns,

decoys, blinds, returning at nightfall dangling
         ragged pairs of geese with smoky eyes.
            You navigate the shallows,

raking muck, mired in certainty. At home you slide
         the curved knife into cracks and shuck,
            lustrous flesh exposed.

One night, I'm drifting rudderless, alone, along a muddy
         river full of rocks. Your cry shipwrecks me—
            The sky is just about to fall

inside the stairs! We wake between seasons, dizzy
in thinning light. These days, we compost
leaves and leavings.

Warm in our shells, at dusk we walk into darkness.
Holding hands through gloves, we kiss,
lips thick with balm.

THE YELLOW GLOBES BURST OPEN

Crows browse like undertakers under ceilings of bronze,
yellow, and late green leaves. In the soft generosity of mist,
the moist canopy outlines trees' lightness
in heavy air; cobwebs in shrubs forge steely connections
     transparent
in ordinary light; behind the hedgerow, in damp rising
to our nostrils, leaves rot to dirt trillium-studded in spring.

We tangle in the underbrush of expectations.
Clearing ropes of strangling vines, we separate tasks,
ourselves—one pulls, one bundles; one handles
poison ivy, the other, sumac's brittle furry bones.
Approving his urge for discipline, you picture
the farmer who cleared our plot, enclosing
his bounds with clean stones hauled by placid oxen—
his walls held the margins together. You work to fill
new gaps, while I reinvent the life lost—
columns of sweet corn tasseling furtive fullness,
pumpkins straining toward orange,
apple trees cascading, fruit ripening,
rotting on the ground. His home,
his wife, were never mastered.
You wrestle down the choking bittersweet
that spirals dead and dying trees,
insect-pocked, woodpecker-pecked, if we cared
to look—homes for squirrel, owl. When the yellow globes
     burst open,
brittle mouths with swollen orange tongues, they tell
how words embody trees and leaves, creatures
of stick and stone, flesh and bone.

The ground is regularly uneven in this field. The level tops
of grass and weed fringe its furrows, the farmer's only legacy.
Our neighbors have kindled the year's first fire, smoke
     signals linger

above the valley, residue of the blaze within.
Crows caw, plangent in the wordless air between us,
their bodies shiny night. Their eyes, black holes,
hold captive light.

THE ART OF RESTORATION

His father, a giant man,
made him learn
the art of restoration.
The workshop boasted
racks and racks of screwdrivers,
slotted and torx, Phillips and hex,
and blades for crosscutting
and ripping pine and oak.
Between sips of Scotch
his father measured
his child against
a blunt-edged board,
then switched the screaming
power saw on high—
every cut the perfect length.
The son's job was to watch and wait.
He absorbed the moods
and vagaries of wood, the way
a table leg could double
as a baseball bat or club
in practiced hands.

And now on weekends he mends engines.
In an antique, perfect world
pistons slip in oiled cylinders,
spark plugs fire in order,
and wires are never broken.
He crouches in the tiny cavity.
Expertly, he makes himself small
above a bloom of coil and steel,
grabbing scraps of crimson flannel
torn in nine-inch squares
to mop up drops of grease or beer.

He believes nothing
can't be fixed
in time.

"AS THE SEA DEVELOPE PEARL, AND WEED"

But only to Himself be known / The Fathoms they abide—
—Emily Dickinson

Erect at the end
of the bed, he stares,
demanding—*Who are you?*
Who are you?
Another night he shouts,
his face floats and flames,
she's pressed against the wall,
sucking air. His fist thrusts
beside her ear and opens
a hole in the plaster,
blind black eye.

Her tongue grows thick
from biting it, drowning
his cargo fathoms
deep—*nigger, spic,*
and *jigaboo*, faceless names
that anchor her in muck.

By day, his face abrades
her cheek with every kiss.
She hoards the unmentioned
as a thunderhead holds lightning,
as the child's tongue
seeks her missing tooth,
as the amputee projects
her lopped-off limb, the hand
that cannot grasp.

THE DRINKER'S WIFE

The red-tailed hawk circles wide,
never lands.
Yet she's seen its nest lodged
in the crooked maple, a haven
beyond squirrels or human voices.
And who would dare
disturb the eggs?

The bird spirals up,
down, finding drafts
even in breathless
air, making wind visible.
On the days she sees
them both, she wonders
if, like many birds,
hawks pair for life.

How long can the hawk stay
aloft? The twisted maple lifts
the nest. At its base,
rusty barbed wire bites deep
inside its thickening girth.

STILL LIFE: DIVORCE

A swollen cirrus veil
trails north. For better
or worse, the season's
turned. It's the driest fall
in years. The garden leaves
a stunted seedless cantaloupe
split by frost.

In autumn's caustic changes
I put the flower beds
to rest, and groom
the gravel drive,
start setting bulbs
in a broad ring
fattening for May,
daffodils blooming
in a spring shower.
From an arid sky,
snow falls like rice.

HUSBANDS: WHAT TO AVOID CHECKLIST

The First

He won't cook.
He never dances.
He insists you take his name.
He likes it when you're sexy, but not too sexy.
He buys the right kind of dog, and the right kind
    of car.
He quits smoking before you meet him, and doesn't tell you
    for ten years.
He starts smoking again.
He likes racial slurs, but doesn't use them until after you're
    married.
He uses them frequently, and when you object,
    uses them even more.
He has no friends.
His father abused him.
He likes gin.
He likes vodka.
He loves piña coladas.
His older sister is an alcoholic.
His twin brother overdoses on rum and prescription
    painkillers when he's thirty.

Punches. Walls.

He owns guns, and won't let you touch them.
He owns guns, and won't tell you where they're hidden.

The Second

He's younger. A lot younger.
He's beautiful, not handsome.
He looks in the mirror several times a day.
He loves his own hair.
He dislikes fat, especially on you.
He makes you mix tapes, when that was a thing.
He runs with you . . . at first.
He criticizes your writing and praises your cooking,
    sometimes.
He buys vitamins in bulk that expire quickly.
He complains about his parents being cheap but says you
    can't afford yard help.
He never applies for work that's beneath him.
He wants you to get a second job, though he's never
    worked.
He has needs.
He has wants.
He hates getting screwed by everyone.

Polyamory.

He just wants friends who aren't your friends.
OKCupid, for him.
OKCupid, for you, afterward. He writes your profile,
    before you leave him.

BREAK

No drama,
just a quick skid down
mossy wet steps, a thud,
a hand stuck out.
No snap.
I could still wiggle my fingers,
but couldn't grip
a button, pull up jeans,
dry my hair. I did
everything right, followed
the protocols—rest, ice,
compression, elevation.
Two weeks later,
my doctor shakes her head,
I should have come sooner,
but it's a clean break,
healing in place.
She wants to scan my bones,
asks if I need help.
Doesn't everyone?
And I've sent my wayward
young husband away
for good.

RUNNING

The morning trail's awash
with birdsong and debris
from late spring floods
when the creek overtopped
its lips, now hairy with roots.

In the wake of a marriage
I run to forget
his dark hair, kind hands,
and betrayal's slow drip,
when a loose root upends me
and I go down
hard, holding my head
between my hands,
hoping my skull won't split.

A dull return to vertical
and speed, ignoring
my throbbing hip,
embedded dirt,
and quick sick gut,
but skirting mud,
rock, and stick litter;
later, bruises will bloom.
No tides this far inland,
but the torrent's subsided
to trickle, and a sole wood thrush
flutes his liquid call
that falls like rain
from a blue sky.

BITTERSWEET

Gloves, shovel, iron bar—
I arm myself, combat
these vines that twine
to tree tops, choke
their hosts. The fall
brings ruthless berries
with gold coats
and scarlet hearts.
I dig, and pull, and pile
the wires of orange roots
until the sun drops
and my sweat dries.
No matter that I've lost,
will always lose.
Never giving ground,
I know too well the cost
of simply giving up.

ON SHORE

Slogging up the dunes,
I've reached the island's end.
The strand grows shells,
a few whips of beach grass,
and twisted plum bushes.
Last fall we boiled the fruit
to make a puckery purple jelly.
The tide reverses, marrying
sea and land.

Today, I walk the beach alone,
transparent as the jellyfish
the waves have heaved up,
splendid tentacles askew.
I'm new as water.
Today, the sea will only grant
the dip and lift
of a dorsal fin headed
toward a dim horizon.

On shore, grass sways,
the plums bloom.
I find myself
amazed that things this sharp
and sweet can root in sand.

WHAT THE BIRCH SAID

Earth's the right place for love.
—Robert Frost

Swinging breaks my back.
Black, yellow, white, silver,
I come in many colors,
acknowledge many kin—
alder, hazel, hornbeam.
My sweet sap rivals maples',
my bark soothes sour stomachs,
my heat cheers cold feet.

I am not yours
to subdue or conquer.
Combing the winter wind,
I long outlive you.
My catkins cast a million seeds—
they make you sneeze and weep.
A pioneer, I feed the forest,
burned or green.
I travel smoothly over water.
Though my roots
are shallow, they split
rock. Unswung,
I bend, not break.

III. BEGINNERS

AS IT WAS IN THE BEGINNING

Those clear yeasty mornings, they speak through silence,
　　　stick-thin Adam and gray-haired Eve.
　　　　　　He sips, she kneads, he needs, she tips,

and laughs my dreams to day. I stutter down
　　　the stairs, the clock's gold disk arrests
　　　　　　me, floating back and forth, ticking,

tickling me, an imp who'd hang suspended
　　　on its rim without her bread's allure.
　　　　　　She shows how it mounds

like flesh, dark rye and white, molasses brown,
　　　it's warm and shiny, yields to touch,
　　　　　　when we keep it warm

it grows. Out back she pinches pins on bleached sheets,
　　　he folds stiff lengths into a wicker basket.
　　　　　　I fall face first in crisp spring sun,

roll to green wisps, cool worm-tunneled dirt.
　　　　Then he sinks with me and says this ground's
　　　　　　good as gold, or better—

we can't eat coins, but should give thanks for squash.
　　　She smiles and wanders in to make
　　　　　　a lemon layer cake, that feeds our need

for yellow like forsythia streamers arched
　　　　beside the kitchen door. Before his outstretched
　　　　　　arms I swing, hung

like a pendulum from an apple limb, then come to
        earth behind him striding off
                to find the year's

first innocents, dotting the meadow in clusters
        like good luck. His brown hands cradle flowers
                the way they hold me after

nightmare gallops through my sleep, they curl
        into bunny shadows on the wall—*What's up, Doc?*
                She makes me eat carrots,

they make you good-looking, they open
        your eyes. Her hands are soft and shiny
                as her bread, their lines worn off,

at dark her fingers comb my shock of hair
        and fear, calming them to silk
                beneath a dome of stars.

These spring nights, he walks me to the silver pond
        reflecting sunset's bloody veins.
                He says that peepers sing

and ring like sleigh bells, that spring always winters over.
        His voice glides me on polished parallel
                runners, behind a horse's sable tail

and dappled rump. I'm a princess
        speaking my own story; I'll never kiss
                a frog because they give girls

warts, and probably on the lips. I'm sure I'll stay myself
        forever, forever
                his and hers, world
                        without end.

THE BUILDER
for my grandfather

1. Dusk

In his old age,
he builds boxes.
He planes a curl of pine
elongated as his torso,
his hands push and pull
the sharpened saw, grip
the ash handle of his hammer.
The joints of his hands,
pine roots, apple burl.
The joints of the box
disappearing.

A pause.
Not a rest,
but a thought
of bigger boxes he's created—
porches, houses, barns.
In the coming darkness,
I cannot see the pitch
that spots his twisted fingers,
or the purple veins
that slice across his hands—
but the pine is so white.
Sliding his palms along the edges,
he smiles and says,
I work from can till can't.

2. Grasping

Your hands, black
with rotted cow dung,
speckled with ashes,

cradle the strawberry sets,
trembling. We bow
above them dreaming
of berries, thimbles
of fire, sharp red water
on the tongue.

In your old turquoise wagon
we sing down the turnpike, dissipate
July. Anything will do—
The Old Gray Mare,
she ain't what she used to be;
Charlie on the MTA—*oh he never*
returned, no he never returned,
and his fate is still unlearned,
poor old Charlie. You point
to the great blue heron
fishing across the river—
one delicate claw poised
beneath a graceful teardrop
of feathers. It seems
he's always there,
a caricature of himself.

You approach
as if through water,
your face a map of rivers,
brown and red roads,
your left hand clasps
your severed right forearm,
as if you don't know
where it belongs,
or to whom. Though
there is no blood, the
stump hangs in shreds.
Your four good teeth gone,
your mouth caves in

on itself and me,
you cannot grasp
me, nor I
you.

The accident makes the local paper—

Elderly man killed in head-on
crash—seat belt fails.

A twenty-four-year-old woman was
leaving Dandy Donuts. Passing
on a blind corner, she crossed
the double yellow line. She had no child seat
for her two-year-old son. Both victims
were treated and released.

I'm the only one who cries
at your funeral.

Later, my mother mouths
her childhood's damp betrayals—
bloodshot eyes, shaky
hands, slurred words.
She never knew you.

Heading home, shifting
fingers of snow swirl
across the car's shell
below the arched backbones
of birches. The river's frozen,
but I can still see
our heron's elevated pose,
his devoted beak,
his great blue
questioning curve.

3. His Answer

The Chevy wagon lifts and dips
over hummocks as sun slants
through maples flanking the field.
I may be three, or four.
Why does the sun punch a hole in my eye?
Why do the trees bleed?
Why aren't butterflies yellow now?
As the garden comes nearer,
your copper eyes promise luck—
look. Fringed by shriveled leaves,
the pumpkins rise like scattered suns.
We grip their prickly stems,
wrinkled rounds, lift and load.
Then squash—acorn, butternut,
and your favorite, bumpy Blue Hubbard.
You say their names like talismans.
You raise me to the lowered tailgate,
show how to spread my arms, sure I can stop
an avalanche of gray and gold and cream.

At home we slice a pumpkin, baring
ivory seeds strung tight on amber wires.
Once, as we wandered
through autumn's soundless
explosions, you told me that fall
was for old people,
it let you rest.

VISITATION

The summer's dim beneath the canopy
of hemlock, oak, and beech,
as if we have a fifth season,
cooler than leaves, warmer than bark.
I walk on last year's harvest
of cones and twigs, awaiting
the blaze of August's razor edge.
A pileated woodpecker sounds
his ratcheting call, bouncing
from tree to tree and making me
will him visible—but no luck.
The littler birds announce themselves
in quick leafy vibrations.

I go to the woods to discover
these lives, and others, following
a long-gone grandfather who prized
the pink hepatica, columbine,
dog-toothed violet, and lady's slipper,
mosquitoes be damned. In the hush
I feel a rush, multiple movements
across a mossy span, that leaves me
waiting, wanting a visitation
that I can never conjure
as I wish—his rough green
worker's clothes, burled hands,
subtle eyes that saw through
every screen. At the woods' edge
the trees release their ghosts,
the solid selves of two turkey hens
and a dozen poults, hurrying after.

WEDDING SHOES
for my grandmother

We clean the attic of debris—fifty years of marriage.
You let me dump
your Reader's Digest books,
save stacks of picture puzzles
for when you can't go out.
A feather pillow, stained
and thin, gets thrown.
Your face flushes
in sudden Indian summer.

Together, we confront
grandfather's enormous hoard—
old, new clothes saved
(from what, I almost ask)—
he says they only get more dear.
Socks in all shades
of gray, most without
mates, boxes of unopened
Kleenex for when paper gets scarce,
a hammer he had during the Depression,
nearly new.

In the late heat, we argue
over what goes, when I discover
them neatly paired beneath a chair:
white pointed toes, high heels
that couldn't support a woman half
your size. I ask for them; you pause
and close your eyes, blinded by
the suddenly reddening sun—
They're not worth much, why?

MY GRANDMOTHER CUTS HER HAIR

On Wednesday afternoons, she marches
into the beauty parlor, strides out,
hair stiff as a sergeant.
Less styled than hammered
into shape, it inspires
silence from the hordes
of children at the grammar school
where she marshals needles,
tongue depressors, mothers.

She retires after thirty years
in the trenches, begins
to wear pants with elasticized waists,
even to the store. She consumes
Danielle Steele novels
like brushfire, though
she says *they're too sexy*
for an old lady.
For months, her hair remains
itself, a helmet. I wonder how
she sleeps inside its ridges.

And then one day it's gone,
and in its place a white and silver cap
whose strands announce a truce.
I went to the barber yesterday!
It's cheaper, and I didn't have to wait.
Stylish, don't you think? She elevates
herself to full five feet
and primps. *After all,*
I only have to please myself.

APT TO LIVE

again, for my grandmother

1. Clearing

Gouging the ground, exposing
perennial flowers, I hack
old growth, hear your missing
half tell us—in mid-March
robins and worms are unnatural.
In the west, a storm blooms,
bruised peony.

Outside the nursing home,
a flutter of sparrows funnels.
The vinyl chair uproots
you, your feet can't reach
the floor, though your stem
is straight as my own. You confide,
I'm getting rid of this fucking chair.
I've never heard you swear before.

I imagine the cancer, squirreled away
beside your ovary, a nut, a knot.
When I look up, pink cabbage roses
multiply on paper borders. Today
you've had your toenails clipped.
We talk about your bowels, the tasteless food.
As rain ticks against the pane,
you devour the strawberries I've brought,
instruct me to tell your housekeeper—
Don't give up my time,
I'm apt to live.

2. Testing

They've propped you up
with pills and pillows;
cataracts blue your eyes.
Your voice curves
in a joke—
Last night I thought
I was back at school.
I'd just finished
third-grade TB tests
when I had to go
to the bathroom.
I looked and looked
but it was gone.
When I woke up
I nearly wet the bed.

I'd forgotten those tests,
the stapler snagged
our forearms, leaving
six red pricks per pupil.
I want to say, remember
when I fell, the pony
standing on my arm,
your calm drive here,
how you held my hand
as I went under?
I want to say,
remember when your barn
burned, and I was away?

Your words see me
down the blinding hall—
I'll try to dream of you
tonight. I wonder why
we rarely think of tests

we pass, only
those we fail.

3. Growing

Jagged as a daisy,
your profile's etched
behind my eye, your sunken
mouth rimmed with foam.
The groans grow
as I approach.
They can't be yours,
coming from a shore
so old I hold my breath.
I plunge through
the open door.

The sheet sinks, white tide.
How can it go lower?
A nurse in a tulip print skirt
floats in.
With a fluid hand
she elevates your head.
I'm going to take your pressure,
Mary. Adjusting the cuff,
she squeezes the black bulb,
sounding unknown currents.
I hold one swollen hand, cold.

When I was small you held
a buttercup beneath my chin.
Did I like butter? You chanted,
Mary, Mary, quite contrary,
how does your garden grow?
We'd always sing,
You have to water it, you know.

Cousins clot the room;
the hours long over,
nurses silent, kind,
I say goodbye.
Behind the frothy curtain,
in the next bed
a woman sobs to her daughter,
I'm sorry I can't stop
drinking. I never wanted us
to end like this.

SELF-FORGIVENESS

In late winter woods
sap seeps; still green,
the ferns are flat as maps,
the stones, road signs,
edge a steep path from north
that's streaked with roots.
Roots, my grandfather used to say,
They'll trip you if you don't look out.
But I've learned they bind
the earth together
with their lovely rules.
Zigzagging down, I spook
a doe; her flag flies.
This white's my direction,
lost and found.

WHAT COMES BEFORE A

The evening star
Venus at full
the new moon
in eastern darkness

a silent phone
a fresh-made bed
a clean spoon
and sharp knife

long dark hair
that needs cutting
a spurned touch
a mouth unkissed

a shout, a raised fist
two ex-husbands
a door closed
before it opens

a flower head
fallen in dust
a new book's smell
and uncreased cover

an old friend's smile
a hand reaching
toward a lover
reaching back

what we need
and sometimes get
just-right sweet
not yet tasted

WIND

It started innocently enough,
Tom Kha Gai and fresh spring rolls,
then Panang Curry Chicken
and Green Curry Duck—
a good sign we both relish fowl.
Perhaps the spices' heat
releases us—your PTSD,
my two divorces,
your losses, my crosses.
Then out into the January night
walking and talking across blustery air.
Absurd to think an algorithm devised
by OKCupid's techs might actually
be right about belated lovers—
99% match, 4% enemy
(though we wonder how we score
more than 100%). You offer me
your coat, and I gently decline,
being inclined toward independence,
a warm house and faithful cat.

These many months later
we're climbing Agamenticus
together, and while I'm hardly keen
on hiking, I appreciate wide views.
By the summit I'm steamy
but the gusts rush through
my summery shirt, so
we pull out windbreakers,
my hair uncontrollable,
buffeting my lined face
that you insist on capturing
on camera, over and over.
To celebrate the ascent,
we split a chocolate Easter Bunny,

though it's early June,
and his feet and ears are melting.
Some risks can't be quantified.

How unexpectedly old
becomes new.
Your slender strength
propels us higher,
makes me pant.
The mountain's really just a hill,
but you love seeing so far,
love the wind,
exciting, wild, unsubdued

WAITING
for Alan, on the eve of his 60ᵗʰ birthday

Your plane is late
again, and I forecast
the worst—faulty
GPS, pilot error,
thunder, hail, lightning,
a wayward goose
exploding an engine,
cabin depressurized,
an oxygen mask failing
to descend—
but here you are,
as always, swooping up
from the terminal gate,
grey hair settled
like dove's wings,
lightly lifting
your wheel-less luggage
despite its heavy
readiness for
all emergencies,
even my soaring
panic, which despite
your weariness
you land
as always, with a look,
circling arms
that ground me,
seeing my first gift
that distant
dark December
was waiting for you,

a sudden cardinal
so close
so bright
to finally
alight.

CLIMBING PILOT
At Pilot Mountain, NC

The Little Pinnacle's ragged
shaggy cliff hangs high
above the crooked trail.
You find the top-rope
anchors, drop
the line and wait
for me to yell
it's reached
the bottom,
then rappel
down the face
to preview holds.
I make you go up first
and watch your feet find
cracks invisible to those below.

We climb five times,
five hundred feet, hug
an arête, stem up
a dihedral, then kiss
a roof, jam up
a chimney—words that make
the mountain a house
with endless doors
and windows open.
How far
can the eye really see?

I've never trusted
such fingery holds,
tiptoe edges, though
you say there's no choss
and let me follow
in my own time.

Neighboring climbers
keep falling—
they're on a different route,
maybe harder, perhaps
with less protection.

At nearly sixty-four
I like being
a beginner again
don't mind awkward
moves, though
I'm climbing well above
my realistic level.
When I reach the top
of Dirty Rotten Scoundrel
you snap a pic
to send our friends
and hold hard
with both hands,
carefully belay
while I inch up
Kiss My Ass.

I've never been this high
before, had so much
exposure. Happily,
I'm not afraid
of falling
and starting over.

ELEMENTAL

"I think I was enchanted"
—Emily Dickinson

silver is a precious metal
atomic number 47 embraced
by copper and gold
soft ductile melting
at 961 degrees Fahrenheit
white when mined
brilliant when polished
black when tarnished
the best electrical and thermal
conductor on Earth

my keyboard's contacts
are silver it covers
every mirror
captures images
sees through flesh
my mouth is full
of the amalgam
with volatile mercury

as a noun it means
wealth security
as a verb transformation—
water's slippery skin
oblique sun on new snow
the spring dawn its
ancient symbol the moon
lunacy of light, noon at night

silver shimmers
when it liquefies
like your torso
in darkness—
silver hair silver hands
silver tongue that leaves
a trail of shine

SEX AFTER SIXTY

You think
it's downhill
all the way
and yes
it's a swooping
slalom trail
skirting shrubs
and fir trees
mounting bumps
catching air
landing
breathing
hard and
pushing off
for more speed
heart pounding
intimating
which direction
comes next
and taking in
the long view
till finally
landing in
a blinding
swirling
steaming
swoosh
that makes
you want
to go
again

KIND EXPLANATION

"To speke of wo that is in mariage"—Geoffrey Chaucer
"The Truth must dazzle gradually"—Emily Dickinson

Chaucer's Wife spoke
beyond woe,
past lust,
to superb surprises,
upright delight—
sudden sun that slants
on quiet snow;
ferns' spiky hair,
winter green
among the melt.

Such poems—
like lives, love—
come like lightning,
flash and flush,
write and unwrite
themselves, blinding
and welcome
as a late valentine.

PARTNERS

for Hepsie, and for Alan

She'd worked it into a comedy routine—
her mom with Alzheimer's driving someplace
she couldn't remember, with her dad, shaking
with Parkinson's but memory intact, riding shotgun.
Together they made it work.
Her mother could barely see above
the steering wheel, and the seatbelt
held her father something like still.

Despite my running and your climbing
we're traveling toward a time
when possibilities loom,
when seventy doesn't seem so old.
How did we leap over decades
without noticing the changes,
without looking in the bathroom mirror
and gasping at the stranger
looking back? We're too familiar
with ourselves, each other, the days'
and weeks' nimble somersaults
that end effortlessly
with years eclipsed.

Somehow, my friend's parents
travelled everywhere for years,
one forgetting and taking direction,
the other remembering and directing.
Somehow, they always arrived
at their final destination.

REFERENCES

"Apt to Live" ["Clearing," "Testing," "Growing'], *The Sunlight Press*.

"[The Art of] Restoration," *Sixfold*.

"As It Was in the Beginning," *Yellow Arrow Journal*.

"'As the Sea Develope Pearl, and Weed,'" *Sixfold*.

"Barn Fire," *Northern New England Review*.

"Bertha the Saint," *Ponder Review*.

"Bittersweet," *Willows Wept Review*.

"Climbing Pilot," *storySouth*.

"Differentials," *Beyond Words Literary Magazine* (Germany).

"The Drinker's Wife," *Sixfold*.

"Family Album," *Ponder Review*.

"Family Plot," *Riddled With Arrows*.

"Foremost Builders," *Ponder Review*.

"Going Under," *Reservoir Road Literary Review*.

"Gone Rogue," *Portland Review*.

"Great Aunts," *Litro* (UK).

"Husbands," *Sea to Sky Review* (Canada).

"Living in a Split, 1959," *Speckled Trout Review*.

"On Shore," *Snapdragon: A Journal of Art and Healing*.

"Restoration," *Sixfold*.

"Self-Forgiveness," *EcoTheo Review*.

"Skaters," *Friends Journal*.

"The Sky Is Just About to Fall," *Sixfold*.

"Still Life: Divorce," *Sixfold*.

"Supply Company": *Litro* (NY).

"Swimming at the Salt Marsh," *Willows Wept Review*.

"Waiting," *Caesura: Reset*.

"What Happened in Fifth Grade," *Speckled Trout Review*.

"What the Birch Said," *Stone Poetry Quarterly*.

"Wind," *Quartet Journal*.

ACKNOWLEDGEMENTS

Restoration, like art, takes time. This book is the work of several decades and has benefited from many helping hands and discerning eyes.

Over twenty years ago, Fred Chappell gave my poems some kind attention that propelled them, and me, forward. More recently, several UNCG colleagues have encouraged me to keep writing poetry, among them Emilia Phillips, Jennifer Whitaker, and Terry Kennedy. I'm especially grateful to my friend and colleague Stuart Dischell, who read an early draft of this book, made essential suggestions, and nudged me toward a much-improved version. Stuart gracefully and humorously models a life in, and of, poetry.

I appreciate Elaine Sexton's candid advice about cover art, as well as her fine poetry. Greg Byrd, once my student, has gracefully transformed me into his. Charter Weeks's photography has long moved and inspired me, and I'm profoundly grateful for his gift of the haunting, powerful cover image.

The Skimmilk Farm Writers' Workshop members inhabit nearly all this book's pages. Beginning in the early 1980s, when Marie Harris generously invited me to join the weekly sessions at poet Jean Pedrick's Brentwood, New Hampshire, farm, I've been properly scrutinized, tested, admonished, praised, encouraged, and supported, as we shared writing, food, and friendship under the apple tree or near the woodstove. Though our numbers are now diminished, the work remains plentiful and evocative, as the group has continued to meet monthly at various writers' homes and, more recently, over Zoom. The current regulars challenge and cheer, and I'm ever grateful for their community. Irma Haggerty, Marie Harris, Ellen Hersh, Helena Minton, Kathy Solomon, Elizabeth Knies Storm, and Connie Veenendaal—I aspire to be you all when I grow up. To my former neighbor and swimming partner, Marie, I shout a special thanks, even though you've moved south and our confabs in the water are less frequent.

Alan has been a devoted partner (and unanticipated muse for many of the book's later poems that surprised me). He restores me every day and every night.

ABOUT THE AUTHOR

A New England native with long farming roots, Karen Kilcup has been an educator for over forty years, teaching all over the northeastern US, as well as in England and Switzerland. Her most recent books are *Who Killed American Poetry?: From National Obsession to Elite Possession*, and *Stronger, Truer, Bolder: American Children's Writing, Nature, and the Environment*. Her poetry has been nominated for a Pushcart Prize, and her forthcoming chapbook, *Red Appetite*, was awarded the 2022 Helen Kay Poetry Chapbook Prize. Karen regularly teaches undergraduate and graduate courses in Literature and the Environment. An avid cook, gardener, runner, kayaker, and rock climber, she lives in coastal New Hampshire with the love of her life, Alan.

PRAISE FOR THE ART OF RESTORATION

"Karen Kilcup is, like the titular craftsman of her poem, a restorer herself, if we understand restoration to mean returning a thing to an original, often enhanced state. She does this and more in an electrifying collection of poems that deliver shocks of recognition along currents of history and memory. She keeps the tools of her trade, which are considerable, sharp, wielding them with a skill born of careful attention to detail, a deep connection to the natural world, and most of all, compassion. Kilcup restores in the reader a belief in humanity with all its flaws (nothing/can't be fixed/in time), and maintains a fierce commitment to love no matter the challenges."

—Marie Harris, Poet Laureate of New Hampshire, 1999-2004 and author of *Desire Lines* (2019)

"The title poem in Karen Kilcup's Art of Restoration describes a workshop with "racks and racks of screwdrivers,/slotted and torx, Phillips and hex,/and blades for cross-cutting." Kilcup's medium is words, not wood, but her poems retain a carpenter's precision, tracing multiple narrative arcs across decades of loss and rebuilding. To read Kilcup is to encounter real world objects charged with subtle (but not suppressed) emotions: a tulip-print skirt, a beaver lodge, a pair of wedding shoes, a birch tree, a dead mother's tractor. This is a lucid and marvelous collection, long in the making and worth the wait."

—Angela Sorby, Brittingham and Midwest Book Award winner for Bird Skin Coat: Poems (2009) and Felix Pollak Prize winner for The Sleeve Waves: Poems (2014)

"In this stunning and courageous debut collection, Karen Kilcup's poems rise above childhood sexual traumas and their later manifestations as she slowly climbs—the recurring motif of this book—toward a willingness to accept mature love and restore her lost youth. As her poems ascend toward recovery, she assures us that the spirit is resilient and that eros and love are available at any stage of life so long as one is willing to confront emotional challenges and risk falling. By allowing love to heal and belay her, Ms. Kilcup has reclaimed the voice denied her so long, and in doing so, she reminds us that beautifully crafted language—the meticulously and sometimes painstakingly acquired art of restoration—can shape and control the narrative of one's life and lead to the possibility of a once-inconceivable joy. I am deeply grateful and fortified for having read this book."

—Robert Bernard Hass, Executive Director of the Robert Frost Society and author of *Counting Thunder* (2008)